Jeannette

Jeannette

A mixtape chapbook by Futureman7

CHAD A. HUTCHINSON

Lightfoot
Press

SIDE 1

SIDE 2

ACKNOWLEDGEMENTS

Have you tried just being still?
—Hal

For Claude

[Side 1]

DEF LEPPARD 84

Sweet, *Musikladen* '74 makes me feel like *Hocus Pocus* by Focus.
The Midnight Special version from 1973, with Gladys Knight
introducing them.
Bringin on the Heartbreak usually makes me feel like that.
But they came out and played it acoustic.
I stood up and booed.
When you stood up and booed too, and looked like you meant it
That's how it's supposed to feel.
I like songs with loud guitars that are rockin. I like songs that are
fast. I turn it up all the way.
I fucking hate it when a band plays their songs slow and acoustic
Like they're fucking Winger or something.
Haha. Just kidding.
I fucking love Winger. I just like to get her riled up.
She's got their name on the back of her jacket.
Fuckin Kix doesn't play their songs acoustic and slow
Kix plays their songs fast. And rockin.
Everyone tries to say Scorpions were the best band that day
"Did you get there in time for Cinderella though?" I say
They blew everyone out of the fucking water.
You can say Scorpions. Or you can say Cinderella.
Anyone that says Def Leppard is out of their fucking minds.
People wanna talk about Priest.
Priest wasn't even on that tour, I tell 'em.
Have you seen Cinderella though?
Night Songs. And *Long Cold Winter*.
All that purple. And pink. And long hair.
Cinderella is the best fucking band on the planet.
Def Leppard's drummer only has one fucking arm and he rocks
harder than any other drummer there is; when they don't make
him play those songs all stripped down and slow.
I fucking stood up and booed em. Scared that I'd offended you

When you stood up with me, and booed 'em too -
I fucking knew right then.
We slammed our beers and threw 'em on the ground.
I took your hand in mine, and we weaved our way to the exit,
through the crowd.
Sitting on top of the hood, we drank one more each from the
backseat cooler, and waited for the line of cars to subside.
The parking lot lights glowing a dull orange yellow a thousand
feet up in the air looked like UFOs
The moon was obscured by the clouds and I kissed you.
Dust and gravel kicked up behind us as we flew out of
the parking lot into the night.
It felt like we were in a rocketship.
You're sticking your arm out the window
Feeling the air through your fingers as the radio is blaring.
Your long hair is blowing in the breeze.
You're so fucking hot in your black Scorpions t-shirt
And your stone washed denim jean jacket
That's covered in patches that say Winger
And Cinderella. And Poison.
And one on the back that's a UK flag, and says
"Def Leppard '84"

BUT FUTUREMAN7 HAS TAKEN TWO TWO-STEP LESSONS IN DREAMS OF ONE DAY BE-ING A REAL TWO-STEP CHAMPION

or at least good enough to be confident; every time.

People already are looking

FUTUREMAN7 makes mixtapes and writes things.
He has had no formal dance training.

NEW YEAR'S DAY

YOU KNOW HOW IT says "use or freeze by (a certain date)" on packages of hot dogs and other meat products? If you freeze the hot dogs on that last day, how many days do you have to eat them when you take them out of the freezer? How many bonus days do I get now? If I had a girlfriend I could ask her questions like that. Unless she's a vegetarian. If she's not a vegetarian we'd probably eat all the hot dogs in time though. Unless she doesn't like hot dogs. She probably only loves authentic Chicago style hot dogs. Or hot dogs at the ballpark maybe. For most of my life I only put ketchup on hot dogs. Like a child. It's only recently that I bought mustard and relish for the first time. That relish jar is so little.

If I had a girlfriend she probably would have told me what that sprayer nozzle thing on the kitchen sink was for. It's only in the last year or two that I learned you can use it to spray ranch and other condiments off your plate. It's been a real game changer. I always just pulled it all the way out of the hole and sprayed it around like a water gun. I never once wondered what its actual purpose was. She hates it when I "accidentally" spray her. Sometimes we laugh about it afterwards. Sometimes we DO NOT.

She picks out the music while we're cleaning up. I have suggestions if she needs some. We'd maybe read a little before bed. She still sometimes laughs at my reading glasses. No one else has ever seen me in them before. They are ridiculous looking. So gigantic. She looks kinda ridiculous in her reading glasses too. But I'd never tell her that. Maybe we'd watch one more episode before we went to bed. She's never seen *The Wire*, and I've been wanting to do a full rewatch. I don't like to watch intense things before bed though. It messes up my dreams.

How's my hair look Mike?

You look good girl.

I've never been good at sleeping next to someone, but this weighted blanket has changed everything. I was never good at sleeping period. I'd toss and turn 400 times. I sleep like a baby now. A baby that sleeps soundly at least. Sometimes I only turn over once, and next thing I know it's morning. I tried the weighted blanket last winter but it made me have a panic attack. My brain was a lot weaker then. I've never slept so great in my life.

I wish you'd stop eating so much chips and cereal in bed, she says. "Cereal?" I say. "Well chips at least," she says. I feel like there should be some distinctions. Definitely not Doritos or Cheetos. Obviously. Bugles and Fritos seem safe enough though. Popcorn is questionable. I like it when Bugles say "America's #1 Finger Hat" on the bag.

The nephews used to perpetually be concerned that I didn't have a girlfriend. They don't mention it at all anymore. These days they just want me to get a cat. You can't reason with a cat though. You can't explain to a cat that sometimes you have to stay in bed till eleven while you wait for your energy to recharge. She understands that though. She understands all of it. I told her about it early on. I hadn't ever told anyone about it before. I hadn't figured it out for myself yet. There's lots of new thoughts in my head. Prior to this year I would have never once thought about getting a cat. I think about it all the time now. Litter boxes are so gross though.

When the ball dropped I'd put my hand behind her head and kiss her intensely. I'd feel an electric charge in my body. I always do. I mostly hated New Year's Eve for my whole life. There was always such expectations to have fun, and it usually just always made me sad. I started loving it right before I met her though. I put on my sunglasses that say "LET'S PARTY" and I am ready.

In the morning when she wakes up I wish her a Happy New Year. I wake up early sometimes. Sometimes I'm rowdy in the morning. Afterwards we'd drink mimosas. I love mimosas but don't usually drink 'em by myself. I mostly only love half a bottle of champagne. She and I'd go through two bottles though. And be sad we didn't have a third. We'd listen to David Childers sing about New Year's Day at the seaside bar. And Slaid Cleaves sing about swimming in Barton Springs. I'd tell her how I only jumped in Barton Spring once on New Year's Day, and how Slaid and Graham Weber were just getting out of the water when I got there. I'd tell her how magical it was. I'd tell her I was so scared I'd have a heart attack when I jumped in, but that it was actually refreshing, and I could totally see why people did it. I'd tell her how I changed clothes in that weird open air changing room and then met Lester at Freddie's Place for bloody marys afterwards. I'd get choked up when I talked about Lester. She knows that I always do. She knows I cry all the time when I feel things these days. It's damn dusty in here this morning, I'd say. And then I'd get back to making mimosas.

Maybe we'd drink bloody marys instead. I don't ever make bloody marys for just me, but we've come up with our own recipe. She fries up some bacon and we add a little Old Bay. I've never cooked bacon in my life. That grease scares me.

I make us some breakfast tacos to tide us over till brunch. I'm still wearing my plastic top hat from last night. The dog stands beside me the whole time. He knows that I'll give him a few bites of egg once they're done. Eggs are good for dogs. I don't know where the cat is. He's probably laying in that ray of sun that comes through the front window this time of day. Sometimes I read there in the mornings if I get up early enough. Sometimes I stay in bed for a while and let my mind wander.

SILVER

THE TRADING POST, "that little store across from where Pa and Ma used to live," has great barbeque now, my dad said. He said it was even better than Smoked.

"Better than Smoked?" I said. "Awesome!" I didn't believe him, but new barbeque is always exciting.

My grandparents lived fifteen minutes south of us. Not far at all, but it felt like a different world. It felt like the country. When I stayed with them we'd have to get dressed up to "go to town." That always confused me - town was where I lived. But I'd put on a shirt with a collar and we'd go to Shoneys or the mall, listening to the Oak Ridge Boys on the radio in the car, singing along to *Elvira*.

They had a huge yard. My cousin and I would throw crab apples at the tractor trailer trucks passing by on the highway below. The field next door was full of hay bales that we'd climb. Hay bales with giant spiders in the webs in between, huge black and yellow ones.

We'd shoot guns off the back porch. Not just bb guns and pellet guns. Real guns. Guns that had a kick, and a smell. I can't even remember now which shoulder you hold the gun up to. I close my eyes for a minute to try to picture it, but I can't get it. I have to shut one of my eyes to focus on the target. It's blurry, but for one second it lines up on that notch and I pull the trigger. It kicks hard and my shoulder hurts bad. My granddad laughs. That gun smell is in the air and I like it.

My granddad had hunting beagles in a pen beside his workshop, but they're only there sometimes in my memory.

There was a metal space ship merry go round ride in the backyard. It had four seats, one for each of the grandkids, that extended out from the center, like a pinwheel. Each seat had handlebars and foot kicks. You sat opposite each other, like a criss cross see-saw, and you'd pump your arms and legs and it'd pick up speed. If everyone worked in unison, and pumped as hard as they could it'd get going so fast that the yellow metal legs would start lifting up out of the ground. You could feel it, and if it was on your side, you'd look down and see it, pulling away from the earth. It was terrifying and exhilarating.

Someone would always stop pumping then. If they hadn't we woulda flown off into the sky - straight into the stratosphere.

My great uncle and aunt drove down from Oklahoma every summer. He'd park his big truck in front of the basketball hoop, next to the tire swing. He had one of those *Dukes of Hazzard* horns on his truck. You're not supposed to talk about *Dukes of Hazzard* anymore, but it was my favorite thing in the world back then. I watched it every Friday night on the TV. *Dallas* came on immediately after, and we'd have to turn it off then, but those first few seconds of images and sounds from the opening theme are somewhere in the back of my brain. I can see them passing by. I'd sit out in his truck and press that button and make his horn play *Dixie* over and over till they'd come outside and make me stop.

My cousin and I laid perfectly still out in the front yard one day, watching a buzzard flying above. We made dying animal sounds to try to get him to come closer. It circled around and around, getting lower and lower each time he passed by. We held our breath and waited. He looped back and all of a sudden he was just barely above the roof of the house, and moving faster. We jumped up screaming and ran inside, slamming the door behind us. My heart was beating out of my chest and I could hardly breathe. My grandparents thought we'd gone crazy.

The undersides of a buzzard's wings are a magnificent silver color that glistens in the sun. A friend one time told me that vultures and buzzards both have that silver coloring underneath, so I don't know which it is. Or maybe she said they're both technically the same thing. Either way, they're both hideous to look at. Except when you're laying out in the grass, looking up at the clouds.

This buzzard is flying a little too low for my comfort level right now though. Last week he was flying real low through the backyards. It made me nervous. I sat in my chair and watched him. He suddenly swooped and landed right on the chimney two houses down. He was huge. It was wild to see.

He's flying even lower than that now. I love that silver sheen, but he is too close. How long has it been since I moved? How long has it been since I showered? I am going to shower today. I'm still alive buzzard!

I get up and go inside to get a snack.

There were always red Coca Cola cans in their pantry. I'd grab a Coke and pour it into one of those white 1970s Thermo Serv glasses. It had old Ford cars on it, Model Ts and stuff. My granddad was a Ford man.

I'd pour the Coke fast, stopping at just the last second, the fizz bubbling up to the brim, almost spilling over. I'd stick my face down in it and slurp it back down. That weird white plasticky insulation felt strange on my teeth. Every now and then I'd pour it a second too long, and it'd bubble all the way up, spilling out over the top. I'd gently lay a Bounty paper towel on top of it. The brown of the Coca Cola would spread across the paper towel like a watercolor.

I can still taste that fizz bubbling up on my nose. It's one of my favorite things. I sometimes try to recreate it now, in a normal glass, but it's never quite the same. If it fizzes enough I can almost get transported back to their kitchen for half a second occasionally. The lighting is always a little dim. It never spills over anymore.

We'd run across the highway to that little store and get Orange Bubblicious bubble gum. Those weird rectangle size pieces with the granules of sugar so big you could feel them in your mouth. The burst didn't last long - sometimes only a few seconds on off days. But it was the best while it did. You could get Hubba Bubba if you wanted to, but it was always Orange Bubblicious for me. Orange Bubblicious and its giant granules of flavor.

"It had lots of bark on it," my dad said, as a follow up. That makes me more intrigued. A good bark can make all the difference.

There's a black and white picture somewhere of my granddad feeding a squirrel peanuts. He's kneeling down and bent over and the squirrel is taking a peanut from his hand. I haven't seen that picture in twenty years probably, but I think about it all the time. I feed the squirrels in my yard grapes. There's one squirrel in particular that really loves them. He comes down the tree and I ask him if he'd like one. I tell him to hold on, and I go inside to get him some. 90% of the time, by the time I get to the top of the stairs and look out the window, he's come over and is sitting directly in front of the basement door. I grab some grapes from the fridge and go back downstairs and outside. I can see him through the door, waiting. When I open the loud door he sits up, with his little paws pressed into his chest, and I toss him the grape. He scoops it up and scurries to a higher location to eat it.

Sometimes he just runs over and climbs to the top of the fence. The fence is only three feet high but it makes him feel better. He sits properly and really takes his time with it. When he's done, he comes down and asks for another. I toss it to him but he'll often try to bury that second one. Silly squirrel, I tell him, you can't bury grapes.

My mom picked up a bag of peanuts from Reid's and gave it to me for the squirrels. Peanuts don't have much nutritional value to squirrels but they like 'em. They're sorta the squirrel equivalent of potato chips. "Hey Squirrel," I say, and I shake the peanuts in my hand. He'll come over and I'll toss him one. Sometimes he'll sit on the arm of the chair next to me while he eats it. And then he'll ask for another. He makes funny sounds when he eats them. We've been doing that for a few weeks. I still have to toss him the grapes, but he'll often take the peanut from my hand now. It makes me smile.

"Pa used to have that squirrel that he fed peanuts," my Dad says. "He'd take em right from his hand. There's a picture of it somewhere."

I don't know if that buzzard really chased my cousin and me, or if we both just imagined it at the same time. The memory of it is all the same. My cousin and I used to throw crab apples at the tractor trailers going by on the highway below, and then we'd run across the street to that little store and get some bubblegum. A buzzard chased us through the front yard one time and we screamed. We'd been laying out in the grass pretending we were dead.

Buzzards are truly disgusting looking; one of the ugliest creatures I've ever seen. When you're lying on your back in the grass though, and staring up at the sky, even buzzards are beautiful to look at when they're flying.

IS THIS IT WYNONNA

They were actually mother and daughter.
But everyone thought they were sisters
at first. At least we all did.

Naomi was so pretty. It was hard to take
your eyes off of her when you were
staring at her singing on the television.

Trying so intently to remember. But I
never could. Which one was the parent
And which one was the kid.

FLEETING (RED)

Sometimes wintertime sunsets. Sometimes
Rainbows in the summertime

And that smell that comes off the
pavement when it rains in July

Foxes and unicorns are both magic
Any time that you see them

DAYS OF KINGS AND PIRATES

I realize the cat isn't with me. And I can't find him anywhere.
I look in my room, and the guest room, and I'm starting to
panic. Which is ridiculous, because he has to be here somewhere.
But this is what my brain does.
In the kitchen, going through the house again, I see that one of
the doors to the under counter cupboards is open just slightly.
The one with all the pots and pans.
I lean down and open it further.
He is sitting very still in the back. Pretending he is invisible -
Like I used to do when I was a kid.
Get out of there! I say with a laugh.
But he waits. In case maybe I'm tricking him.
Only pretending I know he's there.
For he is black and so are the shadows
And always, for his whole life, the ability to disappear when
needed has been one of his magic powers.
THE cat is surprised that the boy can see him, if he really can.
"Let's go outside," the boy says. And that is too much to resist.
Springing and slinking out the cupboard, both at the same time
In that way only cats can do, he races to the front door.
The boy following along behind him.
Both of them excited to start their day.
WHEN the sun is almost up over the tree, that's when the cat
heads to the boy's house. Sitting on the porch till the boy opens
the door.
If he's having a really good morning adventure, sometimes
he forgets to check where the sun is in the sky.

And by the time he sees it, he is late
And he has to run. As fast as he can.
Which is ok, because running is one of his favorite things
Like the boy.
THEY are running through the buttercups in the back lot together.
The cat, like every time they do this, isn't sure if he is chasing
the boy. Or if it's something else that is happening.
But either way he doesn't care.
Just to be doing it is what he loves.
THE cat and I are side by side, bounding towards the tree line.
I don't remember how many years it'd been, before this one,
that I ran just to run.
I am laughing, and there is a gigantic smile on my face.
It feels like Puff the Magic Dragon.
Not the sad part, when Jackie Paper leaves, and he quits roaring.
The beginning, when he was happy and frolicking.
The days when the pirates and kings would bow down when-
ever they saw him.
Hurray, we did it! We yell in celebration when we get there.

CONTRAILS

If you sit inside all day you won't see too many jetstreams.
I saw six or seven this afternoon. The last one, as the sun was
setting, went all the way across the sky and had a faint pink hue.
I stood up to see the end of it.

Fulton loves to sit outside all day and count jetstreams.
He lives a few streets over. He's retired. Blue collar.
Hogwaller accent.
Or maybe Scottsville

Or maybe just old Charlottesville
They're all similar.

He's got one of those big old dinner bells
Like the kind they had in *Lonesome Dove*
Or on the wagon trail.
When he rings it it means it's cocktail hour.

If you hear the bell you're supposed to come over for drinks.
I can't hear it from my house, but I stop by from time to time.
If it's after 4:30 he's usually there.

Fulton drinks Henry Mckenna bourbon and ginger ale.
He calls me Hound Dog sometimes.
I like it when people call me Hound Dog.

One day Fulton saw twelve jetstreams in the sky
at the same time. The most I've ever seen is seven.

I talked to my new neighbors about jetstreams.
They said they'd never seen any since moving
in a year and a half ago.

The next night we all sat out on blankets, in our own
next door yards, and looked for jetstreams together.
It was opening day of margarita season and I went
inside to make us drinks.

When I came back they said I'd missed
two good jetstreams while I was gone.
They said one of 'em was really good
And went all across the entire sky.

I was glad they told me about it.
That's my favorite kind.

10AM NATURAL CHIMNEYS

I want to hear you recite this to us when we are together again, he
said in his email. *I already have this image of walking into your
campsite in the morning before things get rolling, everyone
feeling the effects of the previous evening, good and bad, and you
standing there with a coffee cup of bourbon reading this poem.*

I could smell the bourbon and the coffee.
And could picture exactly in my mind
That slight glare of the morning sun as it rose higher in the sky
And reflected off vehicles and those silver Klean Kanteen pints
That everyone always has.

I could see hungover and weary campers just getting moving
Emerging from their tents
Trudging slowly past us in flip flops
A bath towel draped across their shoulder
On their way to the shower.
Hoping with all all hope that there's any hot water left.

But the cold water will invigorate them
And make them feel alive regardless.

And I could feel it exactly, the sun shining upon us
Secretly gradually warming up the day from the ever
So slight coolness that the night had brought with it.
And without ever fully realizing it happening
It's suddenly become hot outside.

Everyone needs sunglasses now.
Not just me, and my eyes still too sensitive
From the night before. It's so bright
That everyone needs them now.
For a moment at least I can blend in.

People ride by on bicycles; adults and children alike.
People with more energy than I'll ever have.
Bill always says you can't drink all day
If you don't start first thing in the morning.
There's still a couple hours till the music begins.

It's 10 AM at Natural Chimneys campground.
Day two of the festival.

MR. HARTSELL'S RADIO

That taste
throat
and brittle
Submersed
water
Submerged
below you
and some
stems that are
and
reversing
That taste
throat.
time
if your dad
A few more
world inside
An absence
burning low
behind the
you can almost
everything
and out on
with a high
that are
handlebars
Dogwood
that the leaves
pole wires
out of
brick front
Sitting on top

inside your nose
The invisible
veins
Floating
But you can still
and surrounded
Some that are
that are red
rubbery
middle finger
Twirling
inside your nose
Sunset
Stroganoff
got a deer
minutes
A soft
of blue
in the sky
clouds
touch it
Cars parked in
the street
backed seat
bright red
and white
trees
came from
Smoke
chimneys
porch
of the split rail

on the back of your
dust from the crispy
Laying inside them
Like being under
breathe
Orange and brown
yellow
with thick
between your thumb
Twirling and
and reversing
On the back of your
just before supper
Or venison tenderloin
on opening day
It's a whole other
brown cave
The sun
Disappearing
The air so grey
Enveloping
driveways
Big Wheels
Beside tricycles
with chrome
grips
And bigger ones
Telephone
floating
Mr. Allen's
and your own
wooden fence

Watching
calls you to eat
Twirling
dangling
knees
with ridges
Banging
with your
backwards
of your feet
The pile of
driveway
the neighborhood
to see it but you
Streetlights
at the glow
Mr. Hartsell's
in his kitchen
hear it
tonight
in bacon
apple butter
Holding hands
Appleseed
[gross]
Black and silver
And an antenna
Leaf fort
on the wooden
in your mouth

the world
Twirling
Reversing
Husky jeans
Nike sneakers
like dinosaur
the round
heels
and forwards
Forwards
leaves below you
For one whole
turns purple
Faint click
waking up
And the purple
transistor
So loud
outside
And green
Dinner rolls
Ice cubes in
while you
Amen
Rub your hands
radio with a knob
that pulls out
Your heels
fence
That color

till your mom
Reversing
Legs
Reinforced
white and red
teeth
wooden beam
Spinning it
with the bottom
and backwards
next to Mr. Hartsell's
minute
No one outside
Dull buzzing
You stare
is gone
radio
you can
Stroganoff
beans cooked
with brown
water glasses
pray Johnny
Sweaty palms
on your jeans
that turns
all the way
Banging
That taste
grey

ANALOG

It only exists on the Greatest Hits LP, put out in 1979
On the Epic label.
It only exists on vinyl or cassette. It is not streaming
On any platform
For you to click on and instantly hear at 9:30 PM
On a Sunday night
Half stoned.
Half drunk.
Half in love
With the person lying beside you on the couch.
You can only listen to it on a record player
With a glass of bourbon
At the end of side two.
I've spent hours online searching for that version.
I can tell in the first few notes
If it's going to be the right one
Or if it will maybe be close enough
To tide me over. Close enough
Is the best you can get
If you know what the real version sounds like.
The real version only exists on the Greatest Hits
Record from 1979
On the CBS Epic label
On a Sunday night with a glass of bourbon
            Beside a person you're half in love with

PANTHR
(BIG FISH)

Ext. a green grassy lawn with a small stage, covered by a white tent. People sitting on blankets and camping chairs. People dancing. The best rock band is playing. Everyone has a drink in their hand and is smiling. Those outdoor lights that sorta look like Christmas lights, but have bigger bulbs, are strung up around the perimeter, and make everything look like magic. It's a perfect spring evening. The air is cool when the sun goes down. You might be a little chilly if you didn't bring your favorite hoodie sweatshirt. And are just standing still.

"If I'm at a show and having a good time," she said, "but don't know whether it's actually good or not - if I see you there too, then I know that it's real."

"Put your number in here," she said, and he took it and typed it in and handed it back to her.

"Did you put your last name as Panthr?" she asked.

"I wanted to make sure you remembered," he said.

"What's your last name?" he asked.
The light from his screen glowed in the night.

"I'll spell it for you," she said,
"so you get it right."

P -
A -
N -
T -

The boy grinned and she paused.
"Don't get presumptuous and think you know
what the last letters are," she said.

HER

He typed it before she said 'em.

Everyone is on their feet and dancing.
Everyone is smiling. Every single person.
It's a little chilly now that it's dark.
A perfect spring evening.

Those lights that are always strung up outside
In summer that look like Christmas
Lights but with those bigger bulbs
Always make things look like magic
Like that little town in *Big Fish*,
That Loudon Wainwright III was the mayor of.

Steve Buscemi was the friendly town weirdo
The witch lived in the swamp outside of
town and played the piano.

If The Waterboys' *Fisherman's Blues*
Is the last song of the night and you
Don't scream out the high pitched
WOO HOO HOO parts
Every time

Are you even alive?

Light in my head
You in my arms

[w h h]

JACK

THERE WAS A LITTLE SIGN that hung above the front door in his living room all the years that I knew him. Slightly larger than a notecard, about the size of a photograph, it was yellowed from cigarette smoke. A small handwritten piece of paper that said "It's a good life if you don't weaken." That's the thing he said to me the most. That's what he said to me always.

He used to cry all the time. He'd cry about lost loves, and about friends that he'd had that had passed on. He'd cry about his Mama, and how the Mennonites took such good care of her at the end of her life. He got the biggest kick out of the fact that I'd been raised Mennonite, and had identified as one into my early 20's. "A Jack - Mennonite," he'd laugh, "like a Jack Mormon." A wayward Mennonite.

He wore jeans and cowboy boots. He had good hair, and a perfect 70s/80s mustache. He was a true Texan. He always wore his shirt unbuttoned a button or two too low. He was a true Texas ladies man. He'd been married five times. He married two women twice. The third one was a "wild card." He was a self described devout atheist.

He'd tell the story of how when he was fifteen, and living on the border in Harlingen Texas, how one night he brought an older Mexican girl home for supper, and how his Daddy Bob pulled him aside and said "Jackie, your mama don't know it, but that girl's a whore. And you shouldn't bring her into this house."

"And she was a whore," he'd say, through the tears. "She was a Mexican whore and I loved her." And then he'd pause, and sobbing hard he'd say "Shit, she's probably dead now."

He was the guy you'd call if you needed to borrow money. Or needed a ride. Or needed to borrow a tool, or if you needed advice on how to fix something. He peed in cups for his friends on probation, and housed countless "n'er do well shed dwellers" in his workshop/shed if they needed a place to stay for a night or a week or longer. I was even a n'er do well shed dweller for one night after I moved away, and was back in town to visit and had too many drinks to get back to my hotel.

He'd been to 48 of the 50 states. He worked for the circus for many years advancing shows. He'd travel on ahead of the performers and make sure everything was set up in town for when the show arrived. He worked for an oil company for years as well, driving back and forth all across the country. When I moved into the RV park he'd just retired from his final job - a master plumber. He was proud of that.

I had the biggest yard in the RV park, but he had the nicest setup. We'd sit on his porch for hours, drinking and listening to music and telling stories. Merle Haggard, and The Stones, and John Prine, and that Emmylou Harris/Mark Knopfler record were his favorites.

He smoked American Spirits and drank box red wine. He loved ice cold Shiner Bock and Lone Star (bottles only please), and occasionally Spaten Optimator if he was really celebrating. He'd had to give up liquor, but he always kept a bottle of bourbon in the freezer for Gailon and me. The three of us and Gus the Pug would sit on his porch every day. He loved that The Gus was named after Augustus Mcrae. *Lonesome Dove* was his favorite book and his favorite movie. He said everything you needed to know in life you could probably learn from Augustus Mcrae.

He'd been a hippie in the Haight in the 60's. Arrested for having a "peench" of weed, he was facing ten years in prison, and to afford his lawyer costs he had to become a drug smuggler. He'd fly bricks of week in his army bag from California to New Mexico, with dryer sheets on top. The scene in NM would always be abuzz when The Grasshopper's shipment showed up. No one ever knew The Grasshopper's identity, but they always celebrated his arrival.

One time when he got off the plane and went to pick up his army bags he noticed a bunch of guys standing around in dark suits and sunglasses. He thought he was busted, that his time was finally up. He lowered his head, and scooped his bags off the carousel, and quickly spun around and knocked right into one of the guys in the suits. Before he could even apologize the guy held out his hand and said "My name's Bobby Kennedy, and I'm running for president."

He hated Rick Perry with a passion. When the Texas governor's mansion burned down in 2008 he was briefly a suspect. Two DPS agents showed up in the RV park one day, and said they had some questions for him. They asked him his whereabouts on the day of the fire, and a few other things, and then Jack blurted out "Shit, I knew Rick Perry was in Europe. If I'd burned it down I'd have done it when he was in it."

When a thief smashed out a window and broke into my girlfriend's home, he was the first person we called after the police left. "Hold tight," he said, "I'll be right there." He showed up twenty minutes later with four Lone Star tall boys. "I thought you might need these," he said. "There were six of 'em, but I drank one on the way, and I'm taking one with me for later." He nailed a piece of wood over the open hole and the next day, first thing in the morning, he and I went to the glass store and replaced the window.

Freddie's Place was his favorite bar. They had great happy hour deals every week day 4 - 7 PM. At 3:59 each day he was parked in the parking spot closest to the front door. On the rare occasion that someone would already be parked in his spot, he'd sulk and be sullen the whole night, or until Casey showed up and gave him a kiss on the cheek, or Clare made him laugh. He almost always bought every round for Gailon and me.

We'd sit on his porch listening to music on his Bose indoor outdoor sound system. Bose was expensive but worth it, he'd say. If it ever breaks you can mail it to them and they'd fix it at cost. He'd mailed it in three times in twenty years. The final time he sent it to them they said they didn't even make the parts for it anymore, and there was nothing they could do with it. He cursed them, and said old man Bose would be ashamed, and would have never allowed it. He'd been to old man Bose's house in Framingham Massachusetts. Old man Bose was a good man, but he'd never buy another Bose product again. There was a long list of places in Austin that he'd never visit if he thought they'd wronged him at some point.

For his 70th birthday my girlfriend and I took him to see John Prine. I told him he needed to be on his best behavior though, because my girlfriend's mom was coming with us too, and she was a nice Catholic woman. He was drunk when we picked him up. But not as drunk as he could have been. We all had the best time at the show. We laughed lots.

He'd totaled five cars. He'd been shot at twice, hit once. "In the war?" I asked. "Jealous husband," he said. "He walked in and she was on top of me. First shot hit the mattress. The second one hit me in my ass as I took off running naked down the street."

There's a memory that I have, that I think about often. Me, and Gailon, and my sister, who was in town visiting, and Jack, at his favorite place. With a couple that we knew who used to live in the RV park. We were sitting in the family section, by the playground, instead of our usual spot at the bar, because the couple's three year old daughter was there. We were all catching up, and she wanted someone to go on the slide with her. She asked her dad first; "not right now baby," he said. "Chad, will you come with me?" she asked, in her teeny kid voice. "Maybe in a little bit," I told her. "I'll go with you," Jack said. And he put out his cigarette and stood up to join her. (She was beaming). The rest of us, sitting at the table under the giant oak trees, busy being grown ups. And there's Jack and Indy, climbing the little ladder to the slide. India squealing with delight as she pushes off. Jack, in his cowboy boots, grinning, with a gleam in his eye, following after. "Again Jackie Joe!" Indy yells, and she races to the top again, and waits for him. All of us laughing, as we watched them. One of those random perfect days. Those kind that seemed to happen so often then. I was that age still where I thought they'd always just keep happening.

His favorite part of *Lonesome Dove*, the part he liked to quote most often, was the scene where Call and Augusuts are sitting on the bank of the river, talking about the place in their life when they'd been the happiest, and Gus yells at Woodrow "It ain't dyin' I'm talkin' about! It's livin!" Jack would always get choked up when he said it.

He used to cry all the time. But only for a minute or two. He'd cry about his Mama, and about friends and animals that had passed on. He cried when Gus the Pug died. He'd cry about how hard it was to love two women at the same time. I always thought that one was a little ridiculous. But I was a lot younger then. I don't think it's so ridiculous now.

When they asked if there was anything I wanted, "Just that little piece of paper," I told 'em. The one about it being a good life if you don't weaken. He hung it above the front door in his living room so he'd see it every day, and remember. It hangs on my fridge now. So I'll see it every day, and not forget.

"You're a good man Chad," he used to say to me, usually after I brought him more wine from the kitchen, "I don't care what they say about you." And then we'd laugh and have another drink.

We used to laugh all the time. Hours and hours on his porch, sometimes till we ran out of beer. And I'd help him out of his chair, and get him up the two steps into his RV. "I appreciate you Chad," he'd always say. Sometimes "I appreciate you" means infinity more than "thank you."

He used to call every holiday, and he'd ask about my parents, and my sister, and how Gus was doing. He'd always ask when we'd be coming back. He always said he was looking forward to it.

Lots of people called him Jackie Joe. I always just called him Jack.

PERSEUS | SUMMER'S END

Sure they're magical to look at, hovering in place
Their wings going a million miles per second.
But have you ever seen one just sit? Just sit there
on a teeniest branch? One that looks like it
couldn't hold any weight at all

I watched one the other night for twenty minutes.
It just sat there. Every now and then it would
stretch out its little wings and point them up
towards the sky, and then it'd put them back down.
It would shake its little tail feather, and swivel
its head around like a robot. Like that weird
little robot bird in *Clash of the Titans*.

When I was a kid I thought *Clash of the Titans*
was a movie about a guy named Clash, who
was from The Titans.

I could watch that bird sitting there forever.
But they never sit still for too long. I love to
watch them fly too. It's all become my
favorite thing.

I'd never had hummingbirds in the yard before.
Every experience with them has been new and awe
inspiring. I hear that they have seasons though. And
this one is almost over. Soon they'll head south for
warmer climates. I'm seeing them less and less.

I'm sitting out in the yard listening to *Summer's End*
by John Prine. I haven't seen that hummingbird in
two full days, and I feel that cool change in the air.
And the restlessness it brings.

I miss those hummingbirds already.

A friend of mine says if there's hummingbirds
in your yard, then you'll be on its route forever.
I hope it's true. I hope I see 'em next summer.
I look forward to it when it happens.

For so many years the only things that
made me stronger were things that gave me a
dopamine rush. Loud rock and roll concerts.
Fast times with friends. A wild and hot night
with someone I desired.

Suddenly, seemingly almost daily, I find
myself redefining who I am. Redefining
what it is - the things that give me power.

I hated that snake lady in *Clash of The Titans*.
She scared me. I've always been scared of snakes.
But then Clash cut off her head and put it in a bag
And flew away on his flying white horse.

Godspeed hummingbirds.
For one brief moment, I'd almost decided it
wasn't worth it anymore - to keep believing.

Then you appeared

FLASH

On evenings when the weather is nice we pull the blanket
over to the fence and we sit and watch the sky change colors.
We count the number of jetstreams that we see flying overhead.
Some nights we see so many that we lose track.

This is the most content I've ever been in my life, I tell him.
An entire adulthood spent on the run, I never knew how
much I needed a forced down time. I used to feel so restless
it'd feel like my chest was going to explode.

The cat nudges my leg and I reach down and scratch his head.
There's still some time left. When it's totally dark we'll stay
out a few more minutes together, and then I'll fold up the
blanket and head inside, and he'll head back to his own house.

See you tomorrow Little, I'll say, and I'll smile, as I do every
night when I tell him goodbye. We'll both hope the sun
comes up fast in the morning so that we can get outside
and do it all over again.

Two pink and silver ones cross each other above the
giant walnut tree in the yard next door. There's a
quick flash as they pass over the disappearing sun.
How many is that now? I ask him.

[Side 2]

FIFTH GRADE

KICKBALL ON THE BLACKTOP. Sleepover parties and soccer games on weekends. Presidential physical fitness tests. Negative 4 on the sit and reach. Zero pull ups. I have a long torso. Tag and races at recess. Tyrone and I are the fastest boys, and sometimes Bobby. Paulette is the fastest girl. And faster than all of us. There's a big wooden structure, with a giant net made out of rope hanging between the two sides, like a ship on the ocean. There's a long beam off the top that you can balance on and walk to the end and jump off. Like a plank. Like you're a pirate. There are see-saws and a rusted merry-go-round with different colors that goes really fast and throws people off into the dirt.

There's a stoplight in the cafeteria that turns yellow when it gets too loud. If it turns red that means no talking. We sit at the back table, me and all my friends. My mom packs my lunch in my Fall Guy lunch box. Potted meat or Budding ham sandwiches. Sometimes apple butter, that soaks through the Wonder bread and makes it soggy and brown and delicious. Barbecue or sour cream and onion chips in a zip loc sandwich bag that doesn't zip but just folds over inside itself. A Little Debbie snack cake for dessert.

They pull the TV cart into the classroom on the first day of the ACC Tournament if Virginia plays the noon or 2 PM game. All the fifth grade classes come watch. They pull in the TV cart for the rocket launch so we can see Christa McAuliffe become the first lady astronaut in space. We've been reading about her. She's a teacher in Florida. We are all so excited, and we huddle around the TV and count down for the blast off.

I try not to think about that.

We have break dancing competitions in the hall on Friday afternoons. Squilly always wins. He can do the centipede and the back spin and the moon walk. He can also do 100 pull ups. We counted once. He could have kept going. He only stopped because he was bored. I can do a pretty good back spin. And the robot. Sometimes I do the centipede to make people laugh.

In gym class Rodney and I talk about Run-DMC. We each have their tape. We do warm ups to Electric Avenue and then play crab soccer or dodge ball. Some days we play with the giant parachute. Those are my favorite days. Everyone spreads out and lines up around it and grabs an edge of it. Then the gym teacher calls out names and you run under it and cross to the other side. When it's my turn to go, I think to myself that I want to stop and stay under there forever. But you have to keep going all the way across. I stare up at the parachute ceiling the whole time.

After everyone has gone, she throws all the yellow foam balls into the middle of the parachute and we bounce them all up into the air at the same time and they fly everywhere. POPCORN!

There are three different fifth grade teachers. My teacher is Mrs. Atwood. She is my favorite teacher. She is tall with brown hair. She writes nice notes in the margins of my weekly journal assignments. She makes me feel calm when I see her. She makes me feel like I'm going to be famous.

A couple kids in class cause problems sometimes. Mrs. Atwood loves them even more. She sometimes gives them rides home from after school activities. She picks them up and brings them to school for activities at night, like the performance that we put on last week. We sang *We Are the World* and *Itsy Bitsy Teeny Weeny Yellow Polka Dot Bikini*. At the end of *We Are the World* we all raised our arms up in the air, and we were all supposed to hold hands. I was standing on the end, next to Karen Weaver, and we just put our hands real close to each other and pretended.

In our classroom there's a reading corner against the one wall by the door. There are bean bags and a shelf with little square books about Michael Jackson and New Edition and Culture Club. The books have bright pictures inside them. There are also books about chameleons and jaguars and other animals. We get one point for every book that we read. We have book buddies who are in first grade, and one day a week they come in and we read with them. My buddy is Noah. He has light blonde hair that's almost white and he is small. He was really shy at first but now we are friends. I like reading with him. I'm always glad when it's book buddy day.

Mrs. Atwood is sick and we have a substitute for over a month. It's Parker's mom, and she is nice too. Mrs. Atwood comes back for a week after Christmas and we are all so excited. We make cards for her and decorations. She is happy to see us. Parker's mom comes back the next week though. We had our first soccer game last weekend. We beat the red team. It's Spring Fling tonight. There's a cake walk and fishing games and a raffle. We race through the halls while our parents talk. It's fun to run down the hallways at night.

We have off all next week. When we come back there will only be two months left. Then we'll be done with elementary school forever.

~ ~ ~ ~ ~

I WON'T REMEMBER a single thing about 6th grade. Or 7th or 8th, or 9th or 10th. I'll make a comeback in 11th grade though, so don't worry about that.

But I remember 5th grade.

Kickball and break dancing. Tug of war out in the field. Running full speed, neck and neck with Tyrone; seeing him out of the corner of my eye, right beside me, both of us breathing hard. Wondering which one of us will cross the imaginary finish line first; looking down and seeing his shoes kicking up dust off the ground. Lunch in the cafeteria, and all my friends arguing over who gets to sit beside me. And a teacher who believed in me, and encouraged me to dream.

~ ~ ~ ~ ~

MRS. ATWOOD COMES BACK for one more day. We are all so happy to see her. She is skinnier, and has extra makeup on her face. She talks softer and quieter than usual. I know but I'm not allowed to tell anyone.

She hugs each one of us, and all the kids say they hope she comes back soon. She says she hopes so too. But I know though. I know because my mom told me. I know she's come back to say goodbye.

I try not to ever think about that.

She was my friend Andrew's mom. And my mom's good friend. Whenever I saw her, she made me feel a warm feeling inside me. She made me feel calm, and happy. She'd write notes in the margins of my writing assignments that made me smile. That made me feel like I was a superstar, and was going to be famous. She made me feel like every single one of my dreams was going to come true.

If you see Mrs. Atwood, tell her all her kids are doing good. Don't tell her about Walter. It's too sad. Tell her I make a comeback, but it takes a few years. Tell her she was my favorite teacher I ever had. I maybe told her that, but I can't remember. There are some things I try not to think about.

Mitch said he got a new Atari game for his birthday. He invited Dave and me for a sleepover this weekend. We're gonna go see *Rocky IV* at the Terrace Triple in the afternoon. Then we're gonna try to stay up all night.

For Audrey Atwood and Noah Comarovschi

THE LITTLE STORY THAT MENTIONS A BLUE TAILED SKINK

I DON'T KNOW IF that's what it actually is. But that's what I call it. Because it's a lizard with blue stripes that are iridescent, and shine in the sun.

It is mid spring, and the golden light at the end of the day is lasting longer and longer. Tonight it has cast all of the neighborhood in a spectacular glow. I close the composition notebook I am holding, and lay it on my lap. I see her notice me and I wave. "Did you see that sunset?" I call out. "It was glorious."

She lives two doors down. She is attractive, late twenties, light brown hair. She is carrying a bag of groceries up the steps to her side door.

"No," she says. And then she asks me what I'm doing.

"I was watching it, and writing a story," I tell her, "but now I'm just sitting here."

"That's not your yard," she says.

"I know," I tell her. "But the people that live here gave me permission to sit in their yard any time I want to, even if they're not here." The view is different from their yard.

"They love you," she tells me.

"I'm glad," I say, "I love them too."

I extend an invitation, and she puts her groceries away, and comes over and joins me. She has brought with her a blanket and a bottle of wine and two plastic cups.

She has a pet tortoise. It's smaller than you might think. She thought she was buying one of those big ones. This one fits in the palm of her hand, and has long legs. She lets him "run" through the grass. He is fast for a turtle. She corrects you if you call him a turtle.

The owners of the house come home and see us out in their yard, and they come out too. They are drinking Coronas, and it's like we're having a picnic. We are all fascinated by the miniature tortoise. One of them asks if they can hold him, and they sigh about how precious he is.

"We all like teeny things on this block," she says, which makes me smile. And I glance over my shoulder to see if he's coming.

Whenever he sees me he freezes, instantly, and looks at me. Then suddenly, like a starter pistol has been fired, he breaks out in a full on sprint towards me. Literally racing as fast as he can, almost on the verge of toppling over. Never slowing down. Like he's scared I'll leave before he gets to me. Or that there's no time to waste. Like every second faster he can be, is an extra second that we'll get to spend together.

That's how I was as a kid.

Ebullient. Exuberant with my joy.

That cartoon Robin Hood movie. Where Robin is a fox and Little John a bear. The song they sing about running through the forest, and laughing back and forth at what the other one had to say.

Catching crayfish and salamanders. Building forts in the woods, and jumps on the street. For your bike. Sleepovers at your best friend's house in the first grade.

When every day was the best day, and you were excited to go to bed at night because you couldn't wait to wake up and see what good things might happen the next day.

I'd forgotten there was ever a "me" that was that way. It'd been so long since I felt like that.

My whole adult life has been just holding on. Holding on until the next really great thing comes along, that will make me feel alive. For a little while at least. Grabbing onto that for as long as I can. Hoping that one of the times when I do, that it'll last. I've never been "just happy." I fight so fucking hard for happiness; since I was 16.

I feel like that Robin Hood song every morning now. Excited to get out of bed and open the front door and let that weird little cat in if he's there. He is always there. He comes in and we lay on the floor for a few minutes, and he just rubs his face on my goatee, over and over. And I laugh.

I cry sometimes thinking about how beautiful it is to be able to feel like this again; for the past twenty five years I've just accepted that maybe it wasn't possible for me to ever actually feel like that anymore. That maybe, for a person like me, those bursts of happiness were all it could ever be, for the rest of my life. I had come to terms with that. I tried so hard to make those bursts worth it.

Sometimes after I've been thinking about him really intensely, I "come to" out of my trance and I look up, and he's right there. Just appeared out of nowhere. Like magic. I like it when that happens. But it doesn't tonight. He might already be in for the night. This turtle would really blow his mind, I say, and everyone laughs. A Corona is offered to me and I take it. It is cold, and has that Corona taste. There are no limes.

Me and the couple with the Coronas have been neighbors for two years. For the first year and a half we never spoke to each other. We waved a few times but that was it. Now they text me pictures of the sunset and clouds if they see good ones and I'm not outside. We have happy hour on their back deck together some evenings now. We take turns reading our favorite poems to each other. We came up with a rule that a good poem should always be read out loud twice.

The first time we ever talked was about him.

I'd just woken up from an afternoon nap, and was heading out back to see if he was there. They were kneeled down, planting flowers on the other side of the waist high chain link fence that separates our front yards. Standing up, and brushing her hands off on her pants, "We saw your cat out here looking for you earlier," the one with the blonde hair said. "He's so cute."

"He's not my cat," I said. "He's just decided that he and I are going to be best friends and I said okay."

"What's his name?" she asked.

"I don't know," I said, "mostly I just call him Little."

Directly above us, one bright star is shining. When it fills in, it will be part of the Big Dipper. More will start popping out soon. The tortoise is taking one last run through the grass. Its mom asks me what the story I'm writing is about, and I tell her it's kind of about blue tailed skinks.

"I don't know what that is," she says.

"Basically just a lizard," I say.

Peeking out of the folds of a crumpled blue tarp on a sunny day, nestled in a pool of water from the previous night's rain, a snake head and lizard head are nearly indistinguishable.

The first skink the panther ever caught was on the opening day of lawn game season.

He deposited it right in the middle of the Kubb court, in between Dave and Bill and I.

I screamed a little bit.

I never knew what it was that he'd been trying to catch for so long. I'd just see him pouncing around. And determined.

I tried to shoo him away, so that I could get the skink off to somewhere safe. Bill and Dave said there probably wasn't any use to that. It was too late for that, they said.

I wish I'd congratulated him instead of yelling; he was so proud. I'd hate it if I squashed his spirit at all.

Oh my god! I finally caught one! the panther said to himself. I can't wait to show that boy.

The panther trotted to the backyard, the slimy thing dangling from his mouth. It felt different than he thought it would. But he didn't dare let go.

Look! I got one! the panther proclaimed excitedly, as he dropped it in front of the boy. The boy yelled a little, which confused him. Perhaps he thinks it's a snake, the panther said. Snakes ARE disgusting.

I'll try to catch him one of those black and yellow things that are always buzzing around and tormenting me, the panther thought to himself.

And he pranced over to the patch of purple flowers where they frequently hovered. Next to the crumpled up blue tarp. That collects little pools of water every time it rains.

WHERE DO YOU GO TO BUY BIRD BATHS LIKE THE ONES THEY HAD IN 1983 THAT SMELLED LIKE A MIX OF SUNSHINE AND WATER AND CONCRETE WHEN YOU WERE STANDING BESIDE THEM ON A NICE DAY

You got your news in the morning. Sitting at the table reading the newspaper. And again at 6 PM. On channel 4; or 3. The rest of the day was yours. If someone wanted to reach you they had to call you on the phone in the kitchen. And you had to be home. You were excited to check the mail because sometimes your friends wrote you letters. On the second to last page of the paper, by the comics, you'd check to see what was going to be on TV that night, so you could plan for it.

Sunday nights was *The Wonderful World of Disney*.

You'd ride out to the mall with your dad after supper. He'd always see somebody he knew at Sears. Someone he worked with. Or one of your friend's parents. Or a person from church, or somebody he knew when he was a kid. You'd stand politely for a few minutes while they talked. Then you'd ask your dad if you could go to the arcade, and he'd reach into his pocket and give you a handful of quarters, or a dollar for the change machine. Flashing lights. Loud noises. Dark. How happy it always made you, being in there. Your dad would come get you when he was done. You'd maybe get a hot fudge sundae from McDonalds before you left. Or a chocolate milkshake. Sipping on it as you walked back through the mall.

There were two rides by the exit, right before you went outside. A rocketship and a racecar. Until you got too big, your dad would give you one more quarter, and you'd climb up into the seat, adjusting your arms and legs, to get them just right. You'd bend over and insert the 25 cents, listening for it to thunk. Then you'd grab the wheel and hold on tight.

It'd jerk back and forth, real slow at first, and then it'd blast off. Like you were really flying. Tilting forwards, and backwards. Leaning all the way to one side, and then the other. Going and going, hurtling across the galaxy. Sometimes it'd seem like it'd maybe gotten broken. That it was never gonna actually turn off.

Sitting up front on the way home, beside your dad. Passing by the orange Putt Putt on your left. The last colors of daylight slowly disappearing into the night. Staring out the window, replaying it all. Dreaming already of the time you just had.

Thinking about that rocketship ride.
Wishing it'd lasted just a little bit longer.

DRIVING TO GUATEMALA

A RUN DOWN CINDER block building. A small gravel parking lot in front. The air conditioner hanging in the window dripping nonstop, forming a small puddle in the dust and dirt below. The front door is heavy and opens slowly. The smell of cigarettes greets you instantly.

It's dark inside. A plastic light in the shape of a race car hangs over the pool table in the middle of the floor. Bud Light posters with scantily clad women are hung high on the wall. Neon signs and Christmas lights are glowing.

The city outlawed smoking in bars last year. Dee brings over an ashtray and sets it down in front of you when she takes your order. She's thin, with a perm, in her 60s, dressed in nice clothes from a previous era. Polyester pants and a colorful blouse. Straight out of a Raymond Carver story. This is her bar. Dee and Jim's. It is a bar for day drinkers. A quintessential Texas dive bar.

The only natural light in the building is when someone opens the big front door and a wall of sunlight blasts across the floor and pool table. It's always a little startling.

Ice cold beers are $2. You can bring in your own bottle of liquor and buy a 'set up' to mix it with for $3. Black pleather padding is wrapped around the edges of the bar. Like a bumper car. There's a coin operated trivia/photo hunt game on the corner of the bar top. The table at the end of the bar, by the jukebox, is permanently reserved for Dee and Jim. There is no sign to notify you of this.

If you're there in the afternoon someone will probably buy a round of beers for the whole bar. There's usually no more than six people there. Lester will almost always buy a round in return. After a few rounds of free beers I can't keep up. There's already a full beer sitting in front of me. The bartender says she can put me one 'in the hole.' I order a Lone Star and she sets it in the cooler for me. The regulars and Lester will have lapped me at least once by the time I'm ready for it.

Lester always drinks High Life. I meet him at Dee and Jim's sometimes in the afternoons when he gets off work early. It's halfway between the RV park where I live and the house that he and his wife bought recently. Prior to being homeowners they lived in a cool RV, which they sold to me a few months ago. That's how I met him.

Lester is from England. He loves Chelsea fútbol, and his arms are covered in the old style blue/green tattoos. He calls girls "birds" and his friends "mates." He's nine or ten years older than me. He works hard and he parties hard. He charms everyone, ladies and men alike, with his stories and his irresistible smile.

Lester and I have plans. We're going to move to Guatemala in a year. Lester and his wife have lived there before - their daughter was born there. The cost of living is dirt cheap. We're going to buy a small nine room hotel. We'll live in two of the rooms and rent out the rest, catering to American and English tourists. Lester will take care of maintenance and repairs. Kari will take care of gardening and decorating. I will handle online inquiries and guest interactions. It seems totally doable. We've even mapped out a route so that I can drive there in the Wonder Truck since Gus the pug doesn't fly.

Dee and Jim's hosts a Thanksgiving dinner at the bar for all of the regulars. Jim fries up a bunch of turkeys. Dee makes a bunch of sides and pies. It's Wednesday and the bartender is telling us about the feast tomorrow. She emphasizes several times that we should come. It's not just for regulars at all, she says. It's for anyone that wants to come, and anyone who has nowhere else to go.

It's only the second Thanksgiving I've ever missed with my family in Virginia so I go. Lester is busy but Aaron and Ben join me. It's the first time I've ever had fried turkey. The sides and desserts are fantastic. Jim is wearing a baseball cap and untucked striped collar shirt over dark blue Wrangler jeans. He is 6 '3 and almost certainly played offensive line in his youth. He is wearing his standard white sneakers. He comes over and extends his gigantic hand and I shake it. He wishes us a happy Thanksgiving and asks what we thought of the turkey. It's the best turkey I've ever had in my life, I say honestly. Jim is happy to hear that. He says he's glad we're here.

There's talk that Dee and Jim are trying to sell the bar. Someone says they're holding out for half a million dollars. There's new construction across the street. High rise buildings with luxury apartments on top and boutique shops on the ground floor. The neighborhood is changing. They'll probably get it.

Leave some money on the bar. Step out into the light. The sun is just starting to go down. Hurry back to the RV park to let Gus out. He does his business fast and races back in. It's way past his supper time and he's ravenous. He dances in front of his bowl while I scoop him some food.

We never make it to Guatemala. Lester and Kari will get divorced in a few years. The Gus will die a year or two after that. Lester and I will become like brothers. His family is all in England. He says it's nice to have a brother in the states. I only have a sister. Lester is the closest thing I've ever had to a brother. I tell him this all the time.

It's impossible to remain in the RV after Gus' death. There are too many memories, so I sell it. With no place to stay, Lester invites me to live with him for two months. He refuses to accept any money. "I love you mate," he says, "stay as long as you want." I tell him I love him too, but I feel weird about it for some reason. I've never been comfortable saying I love you. Especially to other guys. I don't know why that is. Lester says it freely and easily.

English breakfast in the mornings, complete with HP sauce. Sitting on his porch in West Campus all afternoon, reading books. Through the screen door, listening to my favorite radio station playing on the stereo in the living room, as I watch the people walking by. It feels like I'm living in the Richard Linklater movie "Slacker." When Lester gets off work he will show up with a 12 pack of beer, and we'll drink together all night. His friends from the neighborhood will stop by on their way to the bar and share one with us. They'll invite us to come with them, and sometimes we will.

We talk about our hopes and our dreams. I want to build a tiny home on my property in Virginia. Lester says maybe he'll come in the summer and help me. Lester's dream is to buy a sailboat, and sail around the world for a whole year. His daughter is a sophomore in high school, and he won't go until she graduates. She is the most important thing to him. He tells me I should join him for part of it. It makes me nervous to even think about, but it's also an exciting possibility. I get so anxious if I don't have my own personal space without anyone else around. Lester is the only person I don't ever worry about that with.

The days living with Lester will be some of my favorite days. On the last morning of my two months at his house, I wake up early so I can be sure to catch him before he heads out to work. I thank him for everything, and ask him where I should put the key when I lock the door. He shakes his head and tells me to take it with me. "It's yours now mate," he says, "anytime you need it." Then he gives me a giant hug, and tells me he loves me.

Lester will die unexpectedly three years later. I'll get the phone call at my cottage in Virginia, and collapse onto the bed.

But for now we're all still alive, sitting at the bar at Dee and Jim's at 4 PM on a weekday afternoon, making plans to move to Guatemala. It seems like it might really happen. We've mapped out a route so the Gus and I can drive there and everything; Gus the pug doesn't fly. Lester buys a round for the bar and everyone raises their bottles towards him. I'm drinking Lone Star, trying to keep up. I've already got one in the hole waiting for me. Lester, as always, is drinking High Life. I'm laughing at something he's said.

For Lester Kevern

UNDEFINABLE

If indigo is loneliness, what color is that feeling I've
Felt my whole life, that I never knew had a name to it?

I don't ever wonder where it's going
Or who the people on board might be when I see one

I just stare at it flying across the sky leaving a trail behind
And I feel it inside me.

A friend of mine in New York, he says whenever he sees a
Good one, he likes to imagine that I'm watching the same

One flying overhead, wherever I am.

There's a Portuguese word for which there's no translation
In the English language.

It's a feeling of longing for another time or place.
A time or place that might not even actually exist.

But it's not a sadness. It's a wistful nostalgia. A feeling
For which there's no word for in English

"Windfall" by Son Volt makes me feel like that.
The whole "Trace" album actually.

The first time I remember feeling it from a song was as a kid
Hearing Willie Nelson on the radio singing Steve Goodman's
"City of New Orleans."

I tried to capture it on mixtapes with playlists and songs,
Over and over. Trying to convey in some way what it was
That I was perpetually feeling inside me.

If I'd known it had a name, the first seventy eight mixtapes
I ever made could probably have just been called "Saudade."

It sounds different than it's spelled.

When I close my eyes and try to picture it,
What color it might be

Sometimes it's orange.
Sometimes it's purple.

Sometimes it's red; or green
And blowing in the breeze.

Sometimes it's yellow stars and cacti,
Just after sunset.

Sometimes it's a silver streak,
With a trail of white behind it

Slicing across the sky.

Some days I feel like I could sit outside all day,
Watching them fly overhead

Letting that feeling

overtake me

ANTICIPATION
(NOT NECESSARILY NOT CARLY)

I hear her car pull up and I am waiting. I am so excited to see her.
It is taking her forever to park.
I guess I've never seen her parallel park before. Why would I?
I could have I guess. It wouldn't be that odd, in normal times,
to see someone do that. I've seen lots of people parallel park.
But I don't think I've seen her do it.
I have seen that car parked WAY out in the road before.
I do remember that. That was before I knew them though.
One time I was like
Really? You're not even trying to pretend to be close to the curb.
It made me feel better about my own struggles to successfully
back up in between two cars.
Sometimes I nail it.
But always it's just luck.
Just random chance.
Every single time.
If I don't get it on that first try, sometimes I just close my eyes
and throw it in reverse, and hope for the best.
Sometimes that's all you can do. I always hope for the best.
Especially if I'm downtown.
Especially if I'm downtown and there's a beautiful lady in the
seat beside me. Downtown parking is stupid sometimes.
Not on Mondays probably. Or Tuesdays or Wednesdays.
But those other days. Those other days that I might be looking
for parking downtown and have an attractive lady beside me.
If I don't get it on the first try, then I've either gotta close my
eyes and hope for the best, or I've gotta just drive off and
announce that the spot was too small.
Sometimes I nail it.
She's really stickin' with it.

So many starts and stops.
I'd heard horror stories about kids taking their driving
test when they turned 16 and having to parallel park.
Or maybe I just saw it on the TV.
Kevin might have had to parallel park on *The Wonder Years*.
Or maybe it was one of the Coreys in *License to Drive*.
I'd seen it somewhere. And was terrified to take mine.
But they just made me park in between two straight white
lines in the parking lot. In a totally normal parking space.
Like at a grocery store or a restaurant. I mostly nailed it.
I'm pretty good at that usually. Always have been.
She's still trying.
Good for her.
I'd have given up long ago and just parked up the block.
Left side parallel parking is even worse. Who could ever do that?
Bill likes to tell people:
"There's two things I'm good at. Guess what they are."
It scares people sometimes.
They have no idea what he might possibly say next.
I know the answer. It's not scary. It's parallel parking, one.
And opening jars with lids that are hard to twist off.
Both are true. I've seen it.
Bill always gets the best parking spot.
Opening jars is another something I'm not good at.
I'm totally ok with that.
Except when I can't get that jar open, and no one else is around.
Then I have to get a butter knife and jam it up under the lid.
I've gotta break the seal just a little bit and hope it works.
It's a salsa emergency!
I need one of those flat blue or green rubber circle things that
are always in the kitchen drawer. They're magic.
I don't know where you buy one though.
Or what they're even called.

"Rubber circle gripper thing."

That backing up into diagonal white lines angled the wrong way.

That's the new damn terror.

I don't EVER know what to do with that.

I'll drive around forever instead of park there.

EVERY now and then, if no one is around,

I WILL try it if I'm feeling adventurous.

I'll just close my eyes and throw it in reverse, and hope I nail it.

If I don't get it on the first try I drive off.

She's finally parked! Yay! I've had such a beautiful day and have so many things I've been wanting to tell her. I am ready.

I'm standing on the sidewalk now to greet her.

I'm

Shit. It's not her at all. It's totally someone else.

Shoot. I mean, I'm sure she's exciting too. I don't wanna sound negative about it. I'm sure she's awesome in her own right.

I saw her last week actually, now that I see her.

She was outside on her cellphone.

I yelled across the street and pointed to the sky. "There's a really amazing rainbow behind you if you haven't seen it," I said.

She stood up and turned around. And then went inside and brought that other guy out to show him.

All the while still on her cellphone call.

I was standing in the road taking pictures of it.

It really was an awesome rainbow.

I was hoping she was the kind of person who tells people about rainbows when she sees 'em.

I'm kind of always hoping that everyone is.

I tell everyone about rainbows anyway, just in case.

I always hope for the best.

I'm sure she's lovely and incredibly nice.

I'm sure someone inside was waiting for her tonight, and is super psyched that she's finally arrived.

(It took her forever to park).
She's terrible at parallel parking.
I've had such an incredibly beautiful day today.
I was so excited to tell her about it.

GERRY
[GRANDPA'S FANCY EARRINGS]

THE SIX YEAR OLD nephew is sitting on my lap in the kitchen of my parents' house. On the table is a photo album, full of pictures from when I was pre school age. We are flipping through all the pages, and occasionally I point a picture out to him. Many of these photos I haven't seen in decades. My mind is racing with happy memories.

Midway through we come to a picture that fills me with such sunshine I can hardly contain it. It is a picture of Gerry and my mom and me, sitting on a blanket, having a picnic in the park. There are so many things I want to tell the nephew about Gerry. But I don't even know where to start.

For the first 19 years of my life Gerry Cabell was my favorite person in the world. The love of her life died in the war when she was young, and she never married and she never had kids. When I was born, Gerry just decided that she would love me and dote on me forever.

She worked at the sanitorium with my mom. She was at the tail end of her working career and my mom was just beginning hers, but they became quick friends. Gerry was short with dark skin, and short coarse black hair. She had two cars - a big long Cadillac, and a tan VW bug like Herbie The Love Bug.

She was my favorite playmate. We'd play in my room for hours. She'd sit right down on the floor with me and would come along to every single world I was playing in. If I wanted to be a dragon, she'd be a dragon with me. If I wanted to be a dinosaur, we'd both be dinosaurs. She always smiled so big at me. Her eyes reflected the wonder and magic I felt whenever I saw her.

We'd go to the park and Gerry would ride on the merry go round with me. The fast metal merry go rounds, not the weighted down kinds like they have now. She'd stand and hold onto the metal bars and go in circles with me. I'd watch her and smile. I always felt a warm fuzzy feeling inside me whenever I was with her.

My mom said in the first years after I was born she didn't know how we'd get by. She said they were barely making ends meet with two incomes, and now they were down to just one, and had an additional mouth to feed. She said every time Gerry showed up to play with me she always brought along a bag of groceries. My mom said there were often times when she was so stressed about how they'd possibly be able to cover the bills the next week. And then Gerry would always appear, at just the right time.

Gerry lived an hour south of town in a neighborhood that was all African Americans. We'd go visit her on weekends. My sister and I would play with all the kids on the street, and then my mom would call us inside and Gerry would make a meal for us. Sometimes my sister and I would help her make dessert.

She wore cool pants and cool shirts. There's that scene in *The Blues Brothers* where everyone is dancing out in front of Ray's Music Exchange, shaking it in the street. Gerry looked like she could have been in that scene.

Gerry had different channels on her TV than we did at our house. I was always excited to watch regional NWA wrestling on the television in Gerry's guest bedroom. The Rock and Roll Express and The Road Warriors, and Jimmy Valiant, the Boogie Woogie man. There was a faded brown and white picture on the shelf above the television of a light skinned African American man in uniform. He had a mustache and was wearing a military hat. I'd stare at it when no one was around.

Gerry's bathroom was tiled blue, like it was an ocean, and the soap had a strong smell to it. The toilet paper cover that sat on the back of the toilet was crocheted pink with a little design on it.

One time when I was 11 or 12, for some reason that I can't remember now, I was having a hard day. My parents and sister were visiting with Gerry in the living room, and I had gone back to watch TV. There was nothing on that day but old movies and people preaching though. I went and laid on Gerry's bed and closed my eyes and decided to try to make myself invisible, to disappear for a bit. I squeezed my eyes tight and focused as hard as I could. I just laid there like that for a while. I heard someone coming down the hall looking for me, calling my name as they peeked into the bedroom with the television, where I usually was. I held my breath and squeezed my eyes tighter as I heard the foot-steps come to the doorway of the room I was in. I laid as still as I could on top of the bed. The footsteps stopped in the doorway for a few seconds, and then continued on. "I don't know where he is," I heard someone say. I laid there for a few more minutes, and when I was finally ready to get up I opened my eyes and went out to the living room. "Where were you?" they asked, "we've been looking for you." They assumed I'd been outside playing and had come back in unnoticed. I didn't tell them otherwise.

Gerry would always have drinks and snacks for us. She was always so happy to see us. We never used the front door at her house. We'd knock on the door that was just off the carport, that opened into the kitchen. I'd hear her shuffling across the floor and I'd feel that warm feeling building inside me. Her eyes would be twinkling and she'd be smiling a gigantic smile when she opened the door.

We'd step into her 1970s kitchen, and we'd each give her a hug. I was growing taller and she was shrinking a little bit each time. I used to barely come up to her armpit. Now she barely came up to mine. We'd stand in the middle of the floor and she'd joke and laugh about how she was getting shorter.

We'd all move to the living room, and she and I would sit on the couch together and she'd smile and pat my leg and make me feel important. Then I'd go watch TV while she visited with my parents. My mom said Gerry had experienced horrible unspeak-able acts of racism and prejudice in her life. That made me so sad.

Freshman year of college, my best friend Chris wanted to go see a girl he liked at the women's college 90 minutes away. He didn't have a car, and wanted me to drive him. He said the girl he wanted to see had a roommate that looked just like Nancy Kerrigan, and that I might have fun with her, so I agreed to drive him. Almost to the college we passed the town where Gerry lived. I'd never driven there on my own, only with my parents, but I asked Chris if it would be ok if we tried to find her house real quick. I told him she was my favorite person, and that she'd be happy to see us. In the days before GPS, trying to find a place for the first time on your own was often so much harder than you thought it'd be. Everything looked so familiar though. I found it on the second try. We parked on the street and walked up the driveway and knocked on the side door.

I knocked a few times before she came. For the first time ever, waiting for her, I felt nervous. When she opened the door, I wasn't sure if she knew who I was. "Hi Gerry," I said, "it's me, Chad. This is my friend Chris. We were driving to the college over there, and I wanted to stop by and visit with you for a little." She got a giant smile on her face and gave me a big hug, and invited us in to sit on her couch. She was so small and frail. She was beaming the entire time. She patted my leg and offered us Wild Turkey every ten minutes or so. We would laugh and decline. "We don't need anything Gerry," I told her, "we're just here to see you."

For years after that, Chris would say that we should have just stayed there and drank Wild Turkey and visited with her all night. He said that was the best part of our trip.

At Gerry's funeral my family and I were the only white people there. Her sisters came over and talked to us after the service. And then, one by one, people in the church started coming over to us. We didn't know any of them, but they all shook our hands and introduced themselves. An older couple came up to us, and said they just wanted to say hi, and they talked to us for several minutes. "Can I ask you," my mom said, "how does everyone know who we are?"

"We've heard so much about Gerry's white family for all these years," the man said, "it's so nice to finally meet you."

I didn't go see her at the end, when she was in the hospital. I told myself I didn't want to remember her like that, that I wanted my memory of her to be all of our happy times. I didn't know how to process grief and sadness then, and wouldn't for many years. I know my brain was trying to protect me. But I should have been there.

When I was born, Gerry just decided that she would love me forever, and she did. And I her, with all the capacity as I was capable of. I didn't really understand what love was when I was 19. I just knew how I felt whenever I was with her, how I felt when I looked at her face. I just knew how I felt whenever I thought about her back then - How I feel when I think about her now.

In the picture I am three years old. My mom is so young, with long dark hair, and pregnant with my sister. "Look how different Grandma and I look," I say to the nephew, and he peers in to look closer. "Grandpa looks different too," I add as I point to Gerry.

"His skin looks a lot darker," the nephew says.

"Yeah it does," I tell him, trying not to laugh.

"It looks like he's wearing earrings," he says, and I lean in and study the photograph.

"Hmm...it does look like that," I say. "Go ask him about it."

He carries the open photo album to my dad, who is sitting in the recliner in the living room, and climbs up into the chair with him. "Are you wearing earrings in this picture Grandpa?" he asks.

"Boy, that's not Grandpa!" my dad says, "That's Gerry. She was your uncle's favorite person in the world."

PETRICHOR (TOTORO)

That smell. Of warm summer rain
coming off the pavement; or the dirt.
My favorite smell. My favorite feeling.
An instant flash of nostalgia. I always think four
thousand thoughts about four thousand memories as soon
as I catch the first whiff of it. None are specific.
But always they're pleasant.
Always they consume me.
I try to grab 'em before they slip away
But I can't ever. It is a permanently fleeting saudade.
It's like when you're having one of those awesome dreams.
The kind where you feel it so deeply, and it's so fantastic.
And then you roll over, and you're still half asleep,
Just lying there basking in how good you feel.
You pause for a minute and you start to wake up.
You reach out and try to grab hold of any single image
in your mind that you can see - to try to jump back
into the dream. The images are all blurry though.
And in an instant they vanish.
Every single one. Gone forever.
You can't remember a single thing about the dream at all.
You just remember how good you felt. You can still feel it.
"That smell has a name," the lady in yoga pants said to me.
She was sitting on the ground in the parking
lot watching her daughter ride bicycle.
The clouds in the sky were growing dark.
She said it to my sister actually, I guess.
But I was there. I started the conversation.
"Is that Totoro on your bag?" I asked her.
She said that it was. It hadn't yet started raining
But the sky would open up seven minutes later.
Giant drops, splashing on our arms
As we sprinted to our cars.

JCM

MY MOM JUST CALLED from the hotel. She's super excited. It's their first stop on their bus trip and the hotel gave she and my dad each $30 to spend at the casino, and a $40 voucher for breakfast. She loves free things. I get it honest. My mom said maybe my Dad will win some money on slots. She doesn't say it, but I know she's given my Dad her $30. She doesn't believe in gambling. She won't go into a casino.

My mom doesn't say any curse words. She doesn't drink alcohol or smoke cigarettes. You can say a bad word if it's a quote in a song. "It's a bitch girl, but it's gone too far, cause you know it don't matter anyway..." She sings along to the radio whenever a good song comes on that she knows.

My mom's ears aren't pierced. Her dad, my granddad, was super strict. He disapproved of people defiling their bodies. When my sister wanted to get her ears pierced in the third grade it caused a giant amount of anxiety. My mom had to check the calendar and make sure to schedule it at a time where we wouldn't see my grandparents for two weeks, so that my sister would be able to take out her earrings without the hole closing up.

We got a new Mercury Topaz when I was in the fifth grade. A Mercury Topaz was basically a rebranded Ford Escort, just a different name. It was red and silver. My mom got in trouble with my granddad for buying it because it was so "flashy."

My mom tells the story of how in high school, her dad found a James Brown record in her room, with a half naked lady on the front, and how he smashed it into a bunch of pieces. When my mom came home from school she had to inform him, truthfully, that that wasn't her record, that her friend at school had loaned it to her. When she tells the part about how my Mennonite granddad had to go to the record store to buy a new James Brown record she always starts laughing and has to pause for a minute.

My mom loves rainbows. And P Buckley Moss paintings. If there was a rainbow in the sky, I'd pause my paper route and run home through the yards to point it out to her. On Sunday mornings my mom would always help me assemble my papers to deliver. There's P Buckley Moss paintings on all the walls in my parents' house.

The beach is my mom's favorite place. We had a giant heavy glass bottle, several feet tall and wide. An oversized kind like they build models of ships in and turn on its side. For two years we'd fill it with our loose change. It'd be too heavy to pick up.

At the end of two years, we'd push it over and dump it onto the floor and have a coin rolling party. We'd use the money to go to St. Petersburg beach in Florida. We'd stay in the same place every time. My dad would collect seashells and my mom would take walks on the beach every day. There was a majestic hotel a mile down the beach that was pink, and looked like something from *Gone with the Wind*. The Pink Lady. My mom would walk down to it and stare at it. She'd always buy a postcard with a picture of it. On the off years we'd go to Chesapeake, and stay with her best friend, who she's been best friends with since elementary school. We'd go to Sandbridge beach and set out a blanket on the sand. We'd always eat Pringles at the beach.

My mom's best friend in town was a middle aged African American lady nearing retirement age. She'd come over and play with me all the time. She was my favorite person.

My mom would win every radio contest. Free food, gift certificates, concert tickets, music. She won a set of records from WKAV that was hours of great country songs.

I used to listen to that on the record player. That and a black Johnny Cash record, where he's wearing a headband on the front. It was all songs about Native Americans. Some of the songs would make me sad. But they'd also make me feel something powerful inside me.

Every year on my birthday she'd call into the radio station

before I got up, and while I was eating breakfast, the radio announcer would say Happy Birthday to me on the air. It'd make me feel like I was a movie star. My mom had a book with 100 different cake designs in it. On my birthday I'd get to pick whatever cake I wanted. Race car, bicycle, bunny rabbit, giant pencil. She would make it look just like it did in the book.

My mom sewed curtains for my bedroom when I was a kid. They were light blue like the sky, and had Disney characters on them. I'd sit on the bed and stare at the curtains and dream.

When I was a kid my mom invented a holiday called "Happy I Love You Day." She'd save up her money, and one random day of the year, when my dad would get home from work, she would announce that it was Happy I Love You Day, and she'd give my sister and my dad and I each a gift. It was always something that was exactly what each of us wanted, that somehow she just knew.

My mom and sister and I would walk downtown almost every day. We'd stop at the park and play, and we'd go to the library for story time. We 'd get a handful of books to carry home. Curious George and Ramona and Encyclopedia Brown. Curious George and Ramona were always getting in trouble.

My mom went to every single sporting contest that I participated in from kindergarten through high school. For many of those years it was sports year round. When it was cold she'd sit up in the van with Pat Jensen and watch the game with the door open, sipping coffee. She goes to all the nephews' games now. When it's cold she wraps up in a blanket. My mom would throw baseball with me while my dad was at work.

My mom likes to start her mornings early, before anyone else is up, with a cup of coffee and the local newspaper. The radio is always on in the background. On Saturdays my mom would go to Spudnuts and have donuts waiting for me when I woke up. Once a year on her birthday she would splurge and buy herself either the apple fritter or the bear claw. Every year of my adult life, until Spudnuts closed, I'd go get her a bear claw or apple fritter on her birthday. You had to get there early, they sell out by 10. My mom's birthday in 2016 was the last day Spudnuts was ever open. The last day for a true local institution. I got in line at 5.45 in the morning, for when they opened at six. The line was long. I got the last box of blueberry donuts ever. My mom froze six of them, so that we could thaw them out and have them in the future.

I thought it was a little bit silly, but it was delicious when we did. The nephews still talk about how much they miss Spudnuts.

Most nights of the week my mom cooked dinner for us. She had limited options; my dad wouldn't eat anything spicy or anything with onions or peppers. I wouldn't eat any fruits or vegetables. She'd always find something good to make though. She always did the dishes afterwards. Sometimes we'd go out to eat to McDonalds or Long John Silvers. The McDonalds at the mall had a piano that played itself. The other one had booths that looked like trolley cars. At LJS I'd wear the paper pirate hat on my head and push my cardboard food tray around like a ship. My mom said they loved to go to Long John Silvers because it was the one place I'd always be happy. It was the only place I wouldn't throw a tantrum.

In the second grade I got in trouble for not bringing a 'healthy' snack to school for snack time. I brought Slim Jims and crackers. I told the teacher my mom had packed it for me. My mom had to call the school and tell them that Slim Jims and crackers were indeed my healthy snack, because they weren't potato chips.

My friends in elementary school said they liked to come to my house because there were always sugar cereals and Little Debbie snack cakes.

Christmas is my mom's favorite time of the year. The morning after Thanksgiving, Christmas music is blaring in my mom's kitchen and the oven will be on all day. It will be Christmas music all day every day until December 25. Kenny and Dolly and Boney M and Donna Lou's "Shenandoah Valley Christmas" are her three favorites.

"Donna Lou was your granddad's favorite Christmas album," my mom says.

"I know," I always say.

She sings along loudly and dances to Kenny and Dolly's *I'll Be Home With Bells On*. She always dances and sings along to *Mary's Boy Child*, by Boney M too. When it gets to the rap/reggae part, she will sometimes try to keep up, and then she'll laugh. Anyone playing any Christmas music BEFORE Thanksgiving is something she will get angry about.

My mom hates *Grandma got Run Over By A Reindeer*, but it's my favorite. It's so funny. She thinks it's sacrilegious I think. There was a DJ in Ohio or somewhere who locked himself in the control booth and played it for 5 hours in a row. People went crazy. They had to break down the door to make him stop. He was my idol. For all the years that I lived in Texas, the first time that she heard it every holiday season, she'd call me and hold the phone up to the radio. I'd have a voicemail that was just Elmo and Patsy, singing their holiday classic. Now that I'm back in town, she hates it again. "Merry Christmas Everybody!"

My mom bakes peppernuts at Christmas. Thousands of them. Little bite sized cookies that taste like licorice. The kitchen will smell like that all season. She puts them in small containers and delivers them all over town.

We never had a live Christmas tree. My dad would climb up in the attic and get down our fake one. We'd open the tattered cardboard box and pull out the individual green limbs and the long cylinder "trunk" and the stand. The trunk had holes in it, of different colors- white, blue, orange. We'd find the branches with the right color paint at the end and insert them in the corresponding holes. When you put the last few branches in, it was always kind of magic how it transformed into a real tree. We'd cover it with ornaments, and my mom would put the electric candles in the windows. Pulling into the driveway at night they'd be glowing a majestic orange in the dark, and it'd feel like a movie.

My mom makes little loaves of breakfast breads, in tins, ever since I can remember. My grandma used to make them too. There is always at least one tupperware container of bread on her kitchen table. Blueberry and zucchini are the two main flavors. Apple is my favorite. She has a couple regulars who come to the house every week and buy loaves from her. She sets them out on the porch for them. They like snicker doodle, my least favorite kind.

My mom has been Mennonite her whole life. She used to get upset if she went to church with a friend and they served wine instead of grape juice at communion. For a number of years when I was young we went to a Baptist church. There weren't any kids at the Mennonite church, and my mom wanted my sister and I to have Christian kids to play with. She said Baptists were pretty similar to Mennonites, but they believed in war. Some Sundays the Baptist church would talk about soldiers. We'd try to go to the Mennonite church on those Sundays, or over the mountain to where my granddad was preaching. We were pacifists. My mom didn't like it when I watched *GI Joe*, but I persisted. She said if I got called in to the draft office and had to claim that I was a conscientious objector, that they could hold that against me.

When I stopped going to church my mom continued to invite me, for several years. One day I finally told her, politely, that I wouldn't be going back, so she could stop inviting me. If Christmas is on a Sunday, I might go, for her. Or if her birthday is on a Sunday I might. It's been years since I've gone. My grandma stopped asking me if I'd been to church a long time before my mom did.

Twice a month, in recent years, my mom and I would drive an hour to go see my grandma. My mom would clean my grandma's apartment while I took her grocery shopping. We'd get Dairy Queen for lunch. My mom and grandma would each get a chicken tender wrap and they'd split a small fry. My grandma would always have a coupon for a free dipped cone. She'd always get the complimentary senior citizen coffee. On our drives to Harrisonburg, my mom and I seemed to always have one serious discussion. My mom would ask one question, out of nowhere, about some thing she'd been thinking about. About gay marriage, or the separation of church and state, or things like that. After a lifetime of unquestioning beliefs, I think she was curious that there were maybe other valid viewpoints she was unaware of and should consider.

My mom and I both loved my grandma as much as we loved anything. My mom reminds me of my grandma in a lot of ways. She's always kind, and always trying to help people. She often puts others' needs ahead of her own. I try to encourage her to do things just for herself, to do things just because they make her happy

My mom used to write poems before she had me. She was good at it, my sister says. She stopped writing after I came along. I think it was something that was just a different part of her life. She told me excitedly recently that a poem had just come to her, while she was driving. She said she had to keep saying the words over and over till she pulled into the Roses parking lot and found a scrap piece of paper to write it on.

As far as I know this is the first thing my mom has written since I was born.

Savior (a haiku) by JCM

Maybe with two legs
Maybe four, or black or white
Maybe it's a cat

It is my favorite poem.

I have always known that if I ever needed anything I could ask my mom, and if she was able, she'd help me. For a long time I took that for granted. I thought all moms were like that. I know now that's not true.

People have always said I'm lucky, that good luck seems to follow me. Some of that luck I feel like I helped foster because I always believed in it. Some of it though I had no control over whatsoever.

Whenever *Honky Tonk Women* by The Rolling Stones comes on the radio, my mom turns it up real loud and sings along.

HIS FRAGILE HOPES

He held onto them -

Like a boy of seven wearing shorts
And cowboy boots, running down

The street after the parade
Waving a flag on the fourth of July

Oblivious there's a cost one day.

In front of the grandstand
A senior man and woman in their 80s,

Both wearing nice clothes, danced.
In that intimate animate way

Only old people in love do, that always

makes him feel that thing inside him.
Drinking a beer in the shade as the next

band was playing, he saw them pass
by on the sidewalk in front of him.

The man was holding out his arm,
And she was gripping it tightly. Very

slowly they walked, with small short steps.

Her face, and neck and whole body,
was trembling and shaking

(With thanks to David Childers)

WHEN YOU SEE ME COMING

Miller High Life at the bar. Black label Chapstick.
Levis or Wrangler jeans. Puma suedes and pearl snap
shirts. A walk every morning. To get the blood flowing.
Or in the afternoon if it's too cold. Say hi to all the puppies.
Call all dogs puppy. Ask people how their day is going.
Wish them a happy whatever day of the week it is.
Compliment people on their haircuts and jewelry
and cool sunglasses. Put out hummingbird feeders.
But you have to change the sugar water every seven days!
So? What else to you actually have to do that is so important
that you can't take five minutes out of your day once a week?
Dance in the front row. As hard as you can. Hold your hand
up in the air when you're really feeling it. Be purposeful
with your words. Be kind. Listen to Tom T. Hall and
John Prine. Read Mary Oliver. And *Lonesome Dove.*
Watch *Adventure Time* with your eleven year old nieces
or nephews or offspring. Turn your ringer off. Apologize.
Make mixtapes for your friends. Call someone on the phone.
Tell people how happy you are to see them. Try to go one
whole week without complaining about a single thing.
Then go longer. Lay on your back in the grass and stare
up at the sky. Go outside for the sunset. Learn to trust
your gut instincts - When you can figure out which
ones are trying to save you, and which ones are just
anxiety or preconceived notions that aren't actually
helping you anymore. When the darkness comes in,
remind yourself that it always goes away. Take your
age in years and multiply it by 365. That's the number
of days you've always made it before. Do the things
that you know make you feel good, that at least
give you a chance. Listen to *New York Groove*

by Ace Frehley as many times in a row as you need to.
Question every single thing that you've always accepted
as true. Know that there's many things you were maybe
wrong about. Set boundaries. Be curious. Always
point out rainbows to strangers. Know when to cut it
off. And when to keep accelerating. Extend grace.
Say what you like in bed. Be present. See as much
live music as you can. Take downtime when you need
it to recharge. Listen to your body when it says you
need to stay in. Listen to it when it says you need to go
out. Recognize that a lot of stuff you did was probably
self destructive. Figure out why it happened, and take
control of it. Cheap bourbon on the rocks. 100% agave
tequila. Stocking caps. And fifteen minute power naps.
Overdue fines on the library card. The hard part is
knowing what it looks like. If you just keep asking
yourself "What would the best version of me do?"
And you just keep doing it - Then isn't it you?
If other people see a change in you, and comment
on it - Then isn't it true? When you close your eyes
when you're alone and try to picture what the best
version of yourself would be - What is that you see?
What is stopping you from being it? Look for me
when you see me coming. I'll be looking for you.

JEANNETTE

Bob. Or Gato. Or Little. Or Weirdo. Or Little Weirdo.
Or lately sometimes Little Panther, as he is small and black
and strolls through the grass like a mountain lion.
People want to know if he has a name. Mostly just Little.

Cats don't answer to names anyway. Not like dogs do.
At least none that I've known. This cat loves to chase sticks.
But not like a dog does. You hold onto the stick
and wave it around like one of those cat toys.
The kind that's a stick with a fuzzy thing dangling on the end.
The fuzzy thing is presumably supposed to be a bird.
Cats seem to like that. But this cat likes plain sticks just fine.
The nephews call him Claude.

The cat was wild the first time they met him.
I gave one nephew a stick to shake at the cat. The cat loved it.
He darted back and forth after it, and pounced a few times.
And then suddenly, overcome with madness and excitement,
he leapt up in the air, and stuck his claws in the nephew's knee.
The nephew's eyes got big, and, perhaps holding back tears,
he grimaced, and slowly shouted softly
HE. CLAWED. MY. KNEEEEEEE.

Without hesitation I told him the following
*Claude Ma'nee and his wife Jeannette moved to Charlottesville
from France in 1980. They opened a bakery on Main Street
and served delicious croissants and coffee for thirty five years.*

The nephew looked at me for a moment and then
nodded his head. "Claude Ma'nee," the nephew said.
He pondered it for a minute and smiled. "Claude Ma'nee,"
he said approvingly. And he looked at the cat and asked
"What was his wife's name again?"

EPILOGUE

[MUSIC]

JEANNETTE: A MIXTAPE CHAPBOOK BY FUTUREMAN7

ACKNOWLEDGMENTS

Thank you to Alicia, the Tom Landon hero character to my Beth Macy, for believing in me even when I was crashing. And for everything. IASFIYBB. Thank you to Proal for the many bourbon drinks and support and inspiration. Thank you to John D'earth, and Whitney Matheson, and Jennifer Folsom, and Cecily, and Tim Strong. Thank you to Randall and Dorothy Sommerville. Thank you to my parents, my sister and my nephews. Thank you to Bill and Dave, and Michelle Oliva, and Jon and Brad and Polly and Van and ASS and Beak, and Karen and Claire and Dorothy and Anthony, and Kala and Mina and Rajiva and Clay, and Sherry and Korie and Denise and Sara and the Debbies and Phil and Amanda, and Hsun, and Drew and Lydia and Erin and Karla and Brian and RB and AV. Thanks to Jake and Jeff from Illiterate Light, and Teddy and Sasha and Manoa from Palmyra, Thank you to the Thomas WV crew. Thank you to The Blndrs, and David Wax and Suz Slezak, and Josh Kantor and Reverend Producer Mary and The 7th Inning Stretch 2020, and Sammy and Suzy and Jeff and Spencer Tweedy. Thank you to Jon Byrd and Paul Niehaus. Thank you to Low Cut Connie and James McMurtry and Mary Gauthier and Jaimee Harris and the Maestro. Thank you to Mark Jungers and Adrian Schoolar for all the Texas nights. Thank you to Aaron Wevodau, and Grayon Capps and Lowland Hum and Pete Spaar. Thank you to Richad Will and Adam Larabee and all the Bluegrass Destroyers. Thank you to the mighty David Childers. Thank you to Todd Snider and everyone at the Purple Building for all of the Sunday services. Thank you to all the Transmissionites. I appreciate you.

Next page photo: Craig Shaffer
Front cover photo: W. Randall Somerville

My life is changed forever from knowing you Randall

"Flash" originally published in *The Coneflower Cafe Anthology;* "Terlingua Dinosaur" originally appeared in *Thimble Tiny Lit Magazine;* "Fifth Grade" originally published in *The McNeese Review*

Chad A. Hutchinson is an imagineer and mixtape chapbook artist. He is a born again Virginian, and performs exclusively as FUTUREMAN7 in the Southwest and greater Detroit metro region. This is his first book.

stay strong